The Poetry of Alexander Pc

CW00920950

Volume I

Alexander Pope was born on May 21st, 1688 in London into a Catholic family.

His education was affected by the recent Test Acts, upholding the status of the Church of England and banning Catholics from teaching. In effect this meant his formal education was over by the age of 12 and Pope was to now immerse himself in classical literature and languages and to, in effect, educate himself.

From this age too he also suffered from numerous health problems including a type of tuberculosis (Pott's disease) which resulted in a stunted, deformed body. Only to grow to a height of 4' 6", with a severe hunchback and complicated further by respiratory difficulties, high fevers, inflamed eyes and abdominal pain all of which served to further isolate him, initially, from society.

However his talent was evident to all. Best known for his satirical verse, his translations of Homer and the use of the heroic couplet, he is the second-most frequently quoted writer in The Oxford Dictionary of Quotations, after Shakespeare.

With the publication of Pastorals in 1709 followed by An Essay on Criticism (1711) and his most famous work The Rape of the Lock (1712; revised and enlarged in 1714) Pope became not only famous but wealthy.

His translations of the Iliad and the Odyssey further enhanced both reputation and purse. His engagement to produce an opulent new edition of Shakespeare met with a mixed reception. Pope attempted to "regularise" Shakespeare's metre and rewrote some of his verse and cut 1500 lines, that Pope considered to be beneath the Bard's standard, to mere footnotes.

Alexander Pope died on May 30th, 1744 at his villa at Twickenham (where he created his famous grotto and gardens) and was buried in the nave of the nearby Church of England Church of St Mary the Virgin.

Over the years and centuries since his death Pope's work has been in and out of favour but with this distance he is now truly recognised as one of England's greatest poets.

Index of Contents

The Dying Christian to his Soul

Vital spark of heav'nly flame!
Quit, O quit this mortal frame:
Trembling, hoping, ling'ring, flying,
O the pain, the bliss of dying!
Cease, fond Nature, cease thy strife,
And let me languish into life.

Hark! they whisper; angels say,
Sister Spirit, come away!
What is this absorbs me quite?
Steals my senses, shuts my sight,
Drowns my spirits, draws my breath?
Tell me, my soul, can this be death?

The world recedes; it disappears!
Heav'n opens on my eyes! my ears
With sounds seraphic ring!
Lend, lend your wings! I mount! I fly!
O Grave! where is thy victory?
O Death! where is thy sting?

Solitude

Happy the man, whose wish and care
A few paternal acres bound,
Content to breathe his native air
In his own ground.

Whose herds with milk, whose fields with bread,
Whose flocks supply him with attire;
Whose trees in summer yield him shade,
In winter fire.

Blest, who can unconcern'dly find
Hours, days, and years, slide soft away
In health of body, peace of mind,
Quiet by day.

Sound sleep by night; study and ease
Together mix'd, sweet recreation,
And innocence, which most does please

With meditation.

Thus let me live, unseen, unknown;
Thus unlamented let me die;
Steal from the world, and not a stone
Tell where I lie.

On a Certain Lady at Court, Henrietta Howard, Countess of Suffolk

I know a thing that's most uncommon
(Envy, be silent, and attend);
I know a reasonable woman,
Handsome and witty, yet a friend.

Not warped by passion, awed by rumour,
Not grave through pride, or gay through folly;
An equal mixture of good humour,
And sensible soft melancholy.

'Has she no faults then,' Envy says, 'Sir?'
Yes, she has one, I must aver:
When all the world conspires to praise her
The woman's deaf, and does not hear!

An Essay on Man

Epistle I—Of the Nature and State of Man, with Respect to the Universe

Awake, my St. John! leave all meaner things
To low ambition, and the pride of kings.
Let us (since life can little more supply
Than just to look about us, and to die)
Expatiate free o'er all this scene of man;
A mighty maze! but not without a plan;
A wild, where weeds and flow'rs promiscuous shoot;

Or garden, tempting with forbidden fruit.
Together let us beat this ample field,
Try what the open, what the covert yield!
The latent tracts, the giddy heights, explore
Of all who blindly creep, or sightless soar;
Eye nature's walks, shoot folly as it flies,
And catch the manners living as they rise:
Laugh where we must, be candid where we can;

But vindicate the ways of God to man.

I.

Say first, of God above, or man below,
What can we reason, but from what we know?
Of man, what see we but his station here,
From which to reason, or to which refer?
Thro' worlds unnumber'd tho' the God be known,
'Tis ours to trace him only in our own.
He, who thro' vast immensity can pierce,
See worlds on worlds compose one universe,
Observe how system into system runs,
What other planets circle other suns.
What vary'd being peoples every star,
May tell why heav'n has made us as we are.
But of this frame the bearings and the ties,
The strong connections, nice dependencies,
Gradations just, has thy pervading soul
Look'd thro' or can a part contain the whole?
Is the great chain, that draws all to agree,
And drawn support, upheld by God, or thee?

II.

Presumptuous man! the reason wouldst thou find,
Why form'd so weak, so little, and so blind?
First, if thou canst, the harder reason guess,
Why form'd no weaker, blinder, and no less?
Ask of thy mother earth, why oaks are made
Taller or stronger than the weeds they shade?
Or ask of yonder argent fields above,
Why Jove's Satellites are less than Jove?

Of systems possible, if 'tis confest
That wisdom infinite must form the best,
Where all must full or not coherent be,
And all that rises, rise in due degree;
Then, in the scale of reas'ning life, 'tis plain,

There must be, somewhere, such a rank as man:
And all the question (wrangle e'er so long)
Is only this, if God has plac'd him wrong?

Respecting man whatever wrong we call,
May, must be right, as relative to all.

In human works, tho' labour'd on with pain,
A thousand movements scarce one purpose gain;
In God's, one single can its end produce;
Yet serves to second too some other use.
So man, who here seems principal alone,
Perhaps acts second to some sphere unknown,
Touches some wheel, or verges to some goal;
'Tis but a part we see, and not a whole.

When the proud steed shall know why man restrains
His fiery course, or drives him o'er the plains;
When the dull ox, why now he breaks the clod,
Is now a victim, and now Ægypt's god:
Then shall man's pride and dullness comprehend
His actions', passions', being's, use and end;
Why doing, suff'ring, check'd, impell'd; and why
This hour a slave, the next a deity.

Then say not man's imperfect, heav'n in fault;
Say rather, man's as perfect as he ought:
His knowledge measur'd to his state and place;
His time a moment, and a point his space.
If to be perfect in a certain sphere,
What matter, soon or late, or here or there?
The blest to-day is as completely so,
As who began a thousand years ago.

III.

Heav'n from all creatures hides the book of fate,
All but the page prescrib'd, their present state:
From brutes what men, from men what spirits know:
Or who could suffer being here below?
The lamb thy riot dooms to bleed to-day,
Had he thy reason, would he skip and play?
Pleas'd to the last, he crops the flow'ry food,
And licks the hand just rais'd to shed his blood.
Oh blindness to the future! kindly giv'n,
That each may full the circle mark'd by heav'n:
Who sees with equal eye, as God of all,

A hero perish, or a sparrow fall,
Atoms or systems into ruin hurl'd,
And now a bubble burst, and now a world.

Hope humbly then; with trembling pinions soar;
Wait the great teacher death, and God adore.

What future bliss, he gives not thee to know,
But gives that hope to be thy blessing now.
Hope springs eternal in the human breast:
Man never is, but always to be blest:
The soul, uneasy and confin'd from home,
Rests and expatiates in a life to come.

Lo, the poor Indian! whose untutor'd mind
Sees God in clouds, or hears him in the wind;
His soul, proud science never taught to stray
Far as the solar walk, or milky way;
Yet simple nature to his hope has giv'n,
Behind the cloud-topt hill, an humbler heav'n;
Some safer world in depth of woods embrac'd,
Some happier island in the wat'ry waste,
Where slaves once more their native land behold,
No fiends torment, no Christians thirst for gold.
To Be, contents his natural desire,
He asks no angel's wing, no seraph's fire;
But thinks admitted to that equal sky,
His faithful dog shall bear him company.

IV.

Go, wiser thou! and in thy scale of sense,
Weigh thy opinion against providence;
Call imperfection what thou fancy'st such,
Say, here he gives too little, there too much:
Destroy all creatures for thy sport or gust,
Yet cry, If man's unhappy, God's unjust;
If man alone ingross not Heav'n's high care,
Alone made perfect here, immortal there:
Snatch from his hand the balance and the rod,
Re-judge his justice, be the God of God.
In pride, in reas'ning pride, our error lies;
All quit their sphere, and rush into the skies.
Pride still is aiming at the blest abodes
Men would be angels, angels would be gods.
Aspiring to be gods, if angels fell,

Aspiring to be angels, men rebel:
And who but wishes to invert the laws
Of order, sins against th' eternal cause.

V.

Ask for what end the heav'nly bodies shine,
Earth for whose use? pride answers, "Tis for mine:
For me kind nature wakes her genial pow'r,
Suckles each herb, and spreads out ev'ry flow'r;
Annual for me, the grape, the rose renew
The juice nectareous, and the balmy dew;
For me, the mine a thousand treasures brings;
For me, health gushes from a thousand springs;
Seas roll to waft me, suns to light me rise;
My foot-stool earth, my canopy the skies.'

But errs not nature from this gracious end,
From burning suns when livid deaths descend,
When earthquakes swallow, or when tempests sweep
Towns to one grave, whole nations to the deep?
'No ('tis reply'd) the first almighty cause
Acts not by partial, but by gen'ral laws;
Th' exceptions few; some change since all began:
And what created perfect?'—Why then man?
If the great end be human happiness,
Then nature deviates; and can man do less?
As much that end a constant course requires
Of show'rs and sunshine, as of man's desires;
As much eternal springs and cloudless skies,
As men for ever temp'rate, calm, and wise.
If plagues or earthquakes break not Heav'n's design,
Why then a Borgia, or a Catiline?
Who knows but he, whose hand the lightning forms,
Who heaves old ocean, and who wings the storms;
Pours fierce ambition in a Cæsar's mind,
Or turns young Ammon loose to scourge mankind?
From pride, from pride, our very reas'ning springs;
Account for moral as for nat'ral things:
Why charge we heav'n in those, in these acquit?
In both, to reason right is to submit.

Better for us, perhaps, it might appear,
Were there all harmony, all virtue here;
That never air or ocean felt the wind,

That never passion discompos'd the mind.
But all subsists by elemental strife;
And passions are the elements of life.
The gen'ral order, since the whole began,
Is kept in nature, and is kept in man.

VI.

What would this man? Now upward will he soar,
And little less than angel, would be more;
Now looking downwards, just as griev'd appears
To want the strength of bulls, the fur of bears.
Made for his use all creatures if he call,
Say what their use, had he the pow'rs of all;
Nature to these, without profusion, kind,
The proper organs, proper pow'rs assign'd;
Each seeming want compensated of course,
Here with degrees of swiftness, there of force;
All in exact proportion to the state;
Nothing to add, and nothing to abate.
Each beast, each insect, happy in its own:
Is Heav'n unkind to man, and man alone?
Shall he alone, whom rational we call,
Be pleas'd with nothing, if not blest with all?

The bliss of man (could pride that blessing find)
Is not to act or think beyond mankind;
No pow'rs of body, or of soul to share,
But what his nature and his state can bear.
Why has not man a microscopic eye?
For this plain reason, man is not a fly.
Say what the use, were finer optics giv'n,
T' inspect a mite, not comprehend the heav'n?
Or touch, if tremblingly alive all o'er,
To smart and agonize at ev'ry pore?
Or, quick effluvia darting thro' the brain,
Die of a rose in aromatic pain?
If nature thunder'd in his op'ning ears,
And stunn'd him with the music of the spheres,
How would he wish that Heav'n had left him still
The whisp'ring zephyr, and the purling rill!
Who finds not Providence all good and wise,
Alike in what it gives, and what denies?

VII.

Far as creation's ample range extends,
The scale of sensual, mental pow'rs ascends:
Mark how it mounts to man's imperial race,
From the green myriads in the peopled grass:
What modes of sight betwixt each wide extreme,
The mole's dim curtain, and the lynx's beam:
Of smell, the headlong lioness between,
And hound sagacious on the tainted green:

Of hearing, from the life that fills the flood,
To that which warbles through the vernal wood?
The spider's touch, how exquisitely fine!
Feels at each thread, and lives along the line:
In the nice bee, what sense so subtly true
From pois'nous herbs extracts the healing dew:
How instinct varies in the grov'ling swine,
Compar'd, half reas'ning elephant, with thine!
'Twixt that, and reason, what a nice barrier?
For ever sep'rate, yet for ever near!
Remembrance and reflection how ally'd;
What thin partitions sense from thought divide?
And middle natures, how they long to join,
Yet never pass th' insuperable line!
Without this just gradation, could they be
Subjected, these to those, or all to thee?
The pow'rs of all subdu'd by thee alone,
Is not thy reason all these pow'rs in one?

VIII.

See, thro' this air, this ocean, and this earth,
All matter quick, and bursting into birth.
Above, how high progressive life may go!
Around, how wide! how deep extend below!
Vast chain of being! which from God began,
Natures æthereal, human, angel, man,
Beast, bird, fish, insect, what no eye can see,
No glass can reach; from infinite to thee,
From thee to nothing. On superior pow'rs
Were we to press, inferior might on ours;
Or in the full creation leave a void,
From Nature's chain whatever link you strike,
Tenth, or ten thousandth, breaks the chain alike.

And, if each system in gradation roll
Alike essential to th' amazing whole,
The least confusion but in one, not all
That system only, but the whole must fall.
Let earth unbalanc'd from her orbit fly,
Planets and suns run lawless thro' the sky;
Let ruling angels from their spheres be hurl'd,
Being on being wreck'd, and world on world;
Heav'n's whole foundations to their centre nod,
And nature tremble to the throne of God.
All this dread order break—for whom? for thee?
Vile worm!—oh madness! pride! impiety!

IX.

What if the foot, ordain'd the dust to tread,
Or hand, to toil, aspir'd to be the head?
What if the head, the eye, or ear repin'd
To serve mere engines to the ruling mind?
Just as absurd for any part to claim
To be another, in this gen'ral frame;
Just as absurd, to mourn the tasks or pains
The great directing mind of all ordains.

All are but parts of one stupendous whole,
Whose body nature is, and God the soul;
That, chang'd thro' all, and yet in all the same,
Great in the earth, as in th' æthereal frame,
Warms in the sun, refreshes in the breeze,
Glows in the stars, and blossoms in the trees,
Lives thro' all life, extends thro' all extent,
Spreads undivided, operates unspent;
Breathes in our soul, informs our mortal part,
As full, as perfect, in a hair as heart;
As full, as perfect, in vile man that mourns,
As the rapt seraph that adores and burns:
To him no high, no low, no great, no small;
He fills, he bounds, connects, and equals all.

Cease then, nor order imperfection name:
Our proper bliss depends on what we blame.
Know thy own point: this kind, this due degree
Of blindness, weakness, Heav'n bestows on thee.
Submit. In this, or any other sphere,
Secure to be as blest as thou canst bear:
Safe in the hand of one disposing pow'r,
Or in the natal, or the mortal hour.
All nature is but art, unknown to thee;
All chance, direction, which thou canst not see;
All discord, harmony not understood;
All partial evil, universal good.
And, spite of pride, in erring reason's spite,
One truth is clear, Whatever is, is right.

I.

Know then thyself, presume not God to scan,
The proper study of mankind is man.
Plac'd on this isthmus of a middle state,
A being darkly wise, and rudely great:
With too much knowledge for the sceptic side,
With too much weakness for the Stoic's pride,
He hangs between; in doubt to act, or rest;
In doubt to deem himself a God, or beast;
In doubt his mind or body to prefer;
Born but to die, and reas'ning but to err;
Alike in ignorance, his reason such,
Whether he thinks too little or too much:
Chaos of thought and passion, all confus'd;
Still by himself abus'd or disabus'd;
Created half to rise, and half to fall;
Great lord of all things, yet a prey to all;
Sole judge of truth, in endless error hurl'd:
The glory, jest, and riddle of the world!

Go, wondrous creature! mount where science guides,
Go, measure earth, weigh air, and state the tides;
Instruct the planets in what orbs to run,
Correct old time, and regulate the sun:
Go, soar with Plato to th' empyreal sphere,
To the first good, first perfect, and first fair;
Or tread the mazy round his follow'rs trod
And quitting sense call imitating God;
As eastern priests in giddy circles run,
Go, teach eternal wisdom how to rule—
Then drop into thyself, and be a fool!

Superior beings, when of late they saw
A mortal man unfold all nature's law,
Admir'd such wisdom in an earthly shape,
And shew'd a Newton as we shew an ape.

Could he, whose rules the rapid comet bind,
Describe or fix one movement of his mind?
Who saw its fires here rise, and there descend,
Explain his own beginning, or his end?
Alas what wonder! man's superior part
Uncheck'd may rise, and climb from art to art;
But when his own great work is but begun,
What reason weaves, by passion is undone.

Trace science then, with modesty thy guide;
First strip off all her equipage of pride;
Deduct what is but vanity, or dress,
Or learning's luxury, or idleness;
Or tricks to shew the stretch of human brain,
Mere curious pleasure, or ingenious pain;
Expunge the whole, or lop th' excrescent parts
Of all our vices have created arts;
Then see how little the remaining sum,
Which serv'd the past, and must the times to come!

II.

Two principles in human nature reign;
Self-love, to urge, and reason, to restrain;
Nor this a good, nor that a bad we call,
Each works its end, to move or govern all:
And to their proper operation still
Ascribe all good, to their improper, ill.

Self-love, the spring of motion, acts the soul;
Reason's comparing balance rules the whole.
Man, but for that, no action could attend,
And, but for this, were active to no end:
Fix'd like a plant on his peculiar spot,
To draw nutrition, propagate, and rot:
Or, meteor-like, flame lawless thro' the void,
Destroying others, by himself destroy'd.

Most strength the moving principle requires;
Active its task, it prompts, impels, inspires.
Sedate and quiet the comparing lies,
Form'd but to check, delib'rate, and advise.
Self-love, still stronger, as its object's nigh;
Reason's at distance, and in prospect lie:
That sees immediate good by present sense;
Reason, the future and the consequence.
Thicker than arguments, temptations throng,
At best more watchful this, but that more strong.
The action of the stronger to suspend
Reason still use, to reason still attend.
Attention habit and experience gains;
Each strengthens reason, and self-love restrains.

Let subtle schoolmen teach these friends to fight,
More studious to divide than to unite;

And grace and virtue, sense and reason split,
With all the rash dexterity of wit.
Wits, just like fools, at war about a name,
Have full as oft no meaning, or the same.
Self-love and reason to one end aspire,
Pain their aversion, pleasure their desire;
But greedy that, its object would devour,
This taste the honey, and not wound the flow'r:
Pleasure, or wrong or rightly understood,
Our greatest evil, or our greatest good.

III.

Modes of self-love the passions we may call:
'Tis real good, or seeming, moves them all:
But since not ev'ry good we can divide,
And reason bids us for our own provide:
Passions, tho' selfish, it their means be fair,
List under Reason, and deserve her care;
Those, that imparted, court a nobler aim,
Exalt their kind, and take some virtue's name.

In lazy apathy let stoics boast
Their virtue fix'd; 'tis fix'd as in a frost;
Contracted all, retiring to the breast;
But strength of mind is exercise, not rest:
The rising tempest puts in act the soul,
Parts it may ravage, but preserves the whole.
On life's vast ocean diversely we sail,
Reason the card, but passion is the gale;
Nor God alone in the still calm we find,
He mounts the storm, and walks upon the wind.

Passions, like elements, tho' born to fight,
Yet, mix'd and soften'd, in his work unite:
These 'tis enough to temper and employ;
But what composes man, can man destroy?
Suffice that reason keep to nature's road,
Subject, compound them, follow her and God.
Love, hope, and joy, fair pleasure's smiling train,
Hate, fear, and grief, the family of pain,
These mixt with art, and to due bounds confin'd,
Make and maintain the balance of the mind:
The lights and shades, whose well-accorded strife
Gives all the strength and colour of our life.

Pleasures are ever in our hands or eyes;

And, when in act they cease, in prospect rise:
Present to grasp, and future still to find,
The whole employ of body and of mind.
All spread their charms, but charm not all alike;
On diff'rent senses diff'rent objects strike;
Hence diff'rent passions more or less inflame,
As strong or weak, the organs of the frame;
And hence one master passion in the breast,
Like Aaron's serpent, swallows up the rest.
As man, perhaps, the moment of his breath,
Receives the lurking principle of death;
The young disease, that must subdue at length,
Grows with his growth, and strengthens with his strength:

So, cast and mingled with his very frame,
The mind's disease, its ruling passion came;
Each vital humour which should feed the whole,
Soon flows to this, in body and in soul:
Whatever warms the heart, or fills the head,
As the mind opens, and its functions spread,
Imagination plies her dang'rous art,
And pours it all upon the peccant part.

Nature its mother, habit is its nurse;
Wit, spirit, faculties, but make it worse;
Reason itself but gives it edge and pow'r,
As heav'n's blest beam turns vinegar more sour.

We, wretched subjects tho' to lawful sway,
In this weak queen some fav'rite still obey:
Ah! if she lend not arms, as well as rules,
What can she more than tell us we are fools?
Teach us to mourn our nature, not to mend,
A sharp accuser, but a helpless friend!
Or from a judge turn pleader, to persuade
The choice we make, or justify it made;
Proud of an easy conquest all along,
She but removes weak passions for the strong:
So, when small humours gather to a gout,
The doctor fancies he has driv'n them out.

Yes, nature's road must ever be preferr'd;
Reason is here no guide, but still a guard;
'Tis hers to rectify, not overthrow,
And treat this passion more as friend than foe;
A mightier pow'r the strong direction sends,
And sev'ral men impels to sev'ral ends:
Like varying winds by other passions tost,

This drives them constant to a certain coast.
Let pow'r or knowledge, gold or glory, please,
Or (oft more strong than all) the love of ease;
Thro' life 'tis followed, ev'n at life's expense;
The merchant's toil, the sage's indolence,
All, all alike, find reason on their side.

Th' eternal art educing good from ill,
Grafts on this passion our best principle:
'Tis thus the mercury of man is fix'd,
Strong grows the virtue with his nature mix'd;
The dross cements what else were too refin'd,
And in one int'rest body acts with mind.

As fruits, ungrateful to the planter's care,
On savage stocks inserted, learn to bear;
The surest virtues thus from passions shoot,
Wild nature's vigor working at the root.
What crops of wit and honesty appear
From spleen, from obstinacy, hate or fear!
See anger, zeal and fortitude supply;
Ev'n av'rice, prudence; sloth, philosophy;
Lust, thro' some certain strainers well refin'd,
Is gentle love, and charms all womankind;
Envy, to which th' ignoble mind's a slave,
Is emulation in the learn'd or brave;
Nor virtue, male or female, can we name,
But what will grow on pride, or grow on shame.

Thus nature gives us (let it check our pride)
The virtue nearest to our vice ally'd:
Reason the byas turns to good from ill,
And Nero reigns a Titus, if he will,
The fiery soul abhorr'd in Catiline,
In Decius charms, in Curtius is divine:
The same ambition can destroy or save,
And makes a patriot as it makes a knave.

This light and darkness in our chaos join'd,
What shall divide? The God within the mind.

Extremes in nature equal ends produce,
In man they join to some mysterious use;
Tho' each by turns the other's bound invade,
As, in some well-wrought picture, light and shade,
And oft so mix, the diff'rence is too nice
Where ends the virtue or begins the vice.

Fools! who from hence into the notion fall,
That vice or virtue there is none at all.
If white and black blend, soften, and unite
A thousand ways, is there no black or white?
Ask your own heart, and nothing is so plain;
'Tis to mistake them, costs the time and pain.

Vice is a monster of so frightful mien,
As, to be hated, needs but to be seen;
Yet seen too oft, familiar with her face,
We first endure, then pity, then embrace.
But where th' extreme of vice, was ne'er agreed:
Ask where's the north? at York, 'tis on the Tweed;
In Scotland, at the Orcades; and there,
At Greenland, Zembla, or the first degree,
But thinks his neighbour farther gone than he:
Ev'n those who dwell beneath its very zone,
Or never feel the rage, or never own;
What happier natures shrink at with affright,
The hard inhabitant contends is right.

Virtuous and vicious ev'ry man must be,
Few in th' extreme, but all in the degree;
The rogue and fool by fits is fair and wise;
And ev'n the best, by fits, what they despise.
'Tis but by parts we follow good or ill;
For, vice or virtue, self directs it still;
Each individual seeks a sev'ral goal;
But heav'n's great view is one, and that the whole,
That counter-works each folly and caprice;
That disappoints th' effect of ev'ry vice;
That, happy frailties to all ranks apply'd,
Shame to the virgin, to the matron pride,
Fear to the statesman, rashness to the chief,
To kings presumption, and to crowds belief:
That, virtue's ends from vanity can raise,
Which seeks no int'rest, no reward but praise;
And build on wants, and on defects of mind,
The joy, the peace, the glory of mankind.

Heav'n forming each on other to depend,
A master, or a servant, or a friend,
Bids each on other for assistance call,
'Till one man's weakness grows the strength of all.
Wants, frailties, passions, closer still ally
The common int'rest, or endear the tie.
To these we owe true friendship, love sincere,
Each home-felt joy that life inherits here;

Yet from the same we learn, in its decline,
Those joys, those loves, those int'rests to resign;
Taught half by reason, half by mere decay,
To welcome death, and calmly pass away.

Whate'er the passion—knowledge, fame, or pelf,
Not one will change his neighbour with himself.
The learn'd is happy nature to explore,
The fool is happy that he knows no more;
The rich is happy in the plenty giv'n,
The poor contents him with the care of heav'n.
See the blind beggar dance, the cripple sing,
The sot a hero, lunatic a king;
The starving chemist in his golden views
Supremely blest, the poet in his muse.

See some strange comfort ev'ry state attend,
And pride bestow'd on all, a common friend;
See some fit passion ev'ry age supply,
Hope travels thro', nor quits us when we die.

Behold the child, by nature's kindly law,
Pleas'd with a rattle, tickled with a straw:
Some livelier plaything gives his youth delight,
A little louder, but as empty quite:
Scarfs, garters, gold, amuse his riper stage,
And beads and pray'r-books are the toys of age:
Pleas'd with this bauble still, as that before;
'Till tir'd he sleeps, and life's poor play is o'er.

Meanwhile opinion gilds with varying rays
Those painted clouds that beautify our days;
Each want of happiness by hope supply'd,
And each vacuity of sense by pride:
These build as fast as knowledge can destroy;
In folly's cup still laughs the bubble, joy;
One prospect lost, another still we gain;
And not a vanity is giv'n in vain;
Ev'n mean self-love becomes, by force divine,
The scale to measure others' wants by thine.
See! and confess one comfort still must rise;
'Tis this, Tho' man's a fool, yet God is wise.

An Essay on Man

Epistle III—Of the Nature and State of Man with Respect to Society

I.

Here then we rest; 'The universal cause
Acts to one end, but acts by various laws.'
In all the madness of superfluous health,
The trim of pride, the impudence of wealth,
Let this great truth be present night and day;
But most be present, if we preach or pray.

Look round our world; behold the chain of love
Combining all below and all above.
See plastic nature working to this end,
The single atoms each to other tend,
Attract, attracted to, the next in place
Form'd and impell'd its neighbour to embrace.
See matter next, with various life endu'd,
Press to one centre still, the gen'ral good.
See dying vegetables life sustain,
See life dissolving vegetate again:
All forms that perish other forms supply,
(By turns we catch the vital breath, and die),
Like bubbles on the sea of matter born,
They rise, they break, and to that sea return.
Nothing is foreign; parts relate to whole;
One all-extending, all-preserving soul
Connects each being, greatest with the least;
Made beast in aid of man, and man of beast;
All serv'd, all serving: nothing stands alone;
The chain holds on, and where it ends, unknown.

Has God, thou fool! work'd solely for thy good,
Thy joy, thy pastime, thy attire, thy food?
Who for thy table feeds the wanton fawn,
For him as kindly spread the flow'ry lawn:
Is it for thee the lark ascends and sings?
Joy tunes his voice, joy elevates his wings.
Is it for thee the linnet pours his throat?
Loves of his own and raptures swell the note.
The bounding steed you pompously bestride,
Shares with his lord the pleasure and the pride.
Is thine alone the seed that strews the plain?
The birds of heav'n shall vindicate their grain.
Thine the full harvest of the golden year?
Part pays, and justly, the deserving steer:
The hog, that plows not, nor obeys thy call,
Lives on the labours of this lord of all.

Know, nature's children all divide her care;
The fur that warms a monarch, warm'd a bear.
While man exclaims, 'See all things for my use!'
'See man for mine!' replies a pamper'd goose:
And just as short of reason he must fall,
Who thinks all made for one, not one for all.

Grant that the pow'rful still the weak control;
Be man the wit and tyrant of the whole:
Nature that tyrant checks; he only knows,
And helps, another creature's wants and woes.
Say, will the falcon, stooping from above,
Smit with her varying plumage, spare the dove?
Admires the jay the insect's gilded wings?
Or hears the hawk when Philomela sings?
Man cares for all: to birds he gives his woods,
To beasts his pastures, and to fish his floods;
For some his int'rest prompts him to provide,
All feed on one vain patron, and enjoy
Th' extensive blessing of his luxury,
That very life his learned hunger craves,
He saves from famine, from the savage saves;
Nay, feasts the animal he dooms his feast,
And, till he ends the being, makes it blest:
Which sees no more the stroke, or feels the pain,
Than favour'd man by touch ether'al slain.
The creature had his feast of life before;
Thou too must perish, when thy feast is o'er!

To each unthinking being, heav'n, a friend,
Gives not the useless knowledge of its end:
To man imparts it; but with such a view
As, while he dreads it, makes him hope it too:
The hour conceal'd, and so remote the fear,
Death still draws nearer, never seeming near.
Great standing miracle! that heav'n assign'd
Its only thinking thing this turn of mind.

II.

Whether with reason, or with instinct blest,
Know, all enjoy that pow'r which suits them best;
To bliss alike by that direction tend,
And find the means proportion'd to their end.
Say, where full instinct is th' unerring guide,
What Pope or council can they need beside?
Reason, however able, cool at best,

Cares not for service, or but serves when prest,
Stays 'till we call, and then not often near;
But honest instinct comes a volunteer,
Sure never to o'er-shoot, but just to hit;
While still too wide or short is human wit;
Sure by quick nature happiness to gain,
Which heavier reason labours at in vain.
This too serves always, reason never long;
One must go right, the other may go wrong.
See then the acting and comparing pow'rs
One in their nature, which are two in ours;
And reason raise o'er instinct as you can,
In this 'tis God directs, in that 'tis man.

Who taught the nations of the field and flood
To shun their poison, and to chuse their food?
Prescient, the tides or tempests to withstand,
Build on the wave, or arch beneath the sand?
Who made the spider parallels design,
Sure as De Moivre, without rule or line?
Who bid the stork, Columbus-like, explore
Heav'ns not his own, and worlds unknown before?
Who calls the council, states the certain day,
Who forms the phalanx, and who points the way?

III.

God, in the nature of each being, founds
Its proper bliss, and sets its proper bounds:
But as he fram'd a whole, the whole to bless,
On mutual wants built mutual happiness:
So from the first, eternal order ran,
And creature link'd to creature, man to man.
Whate'er of life all-quick'ning ether keeps,
Or breathes thro' air, or shoots beneath the deeps,
Or pours profuse on earth, one nature feeds
The vital flame, and swells the genial seeds.
Not man alone, but all that roam the wood,
Or wing the sky, or roll along the flood,
Each loves itself, but not itself alone,
Each sex desires alike, 'till two are one.
Nor ends the pleasure with the fierce embrace;
They love themselves, a third time, in their race.
Thus beast and bird their common charge attend
The mothers nurse it, and the sires defend;
The young dismiss'd to wander earth or air,
There stops the instinct, and there ends the care;

The link dissolves, each seeks a fresh embrace,
Another love succeeds, another race.
A longer care man's helpless kind demands;
That longer care contracts more lasting bands:
Reflection, reason, still the ties improve,
At once extend the int'rest, and the love:
With choice we fix, with sympathy we burn;
Each virtue in each passion takes its turn;
And still new needs, new helps, new habits rise,
That graft benevolence on charities.
Still as one brood, and as another rose,
These nat'ral love maintain'd, habitual those:
The last, scarce ripen'd into perfect man,
Saw helpless him from whom their life began:
Mem'ry and fore-cast just returns engage,
That pointed back to youth, this on to age;
While pleasure, gratitude, and hope, combin'd,
Still spread the int'rest and preserv'd the kind.

IV.

Nor think, in nature's state they blindly trod;
The state of nature was the reign of God:
Self-love and social at her birth began,
Union the bond of all things, and of man.
Pride then was not; nor arts, that pride to aid;
Man walk'd with beast, joint tenant of the shade,
The same his table, and the same his bed;
No murder cloth'd him, and no murder fed.
In the same temple, the resounding wood,
All vocal beings hymn'd their equal God:
The shrine with gore unstain'd, with gold undrest,
Unbrib'd, unbloody, stood the blameless priest:
Heav'n's attribute was universal care,
And man's prerogative, to rule, but spare.
Ah! how unlike the man of times to come!
Of half that live the butcher and the tomb;
Who, foe to nature, hears the gen'ral groan,
Murders their species, and betrays his own.
But just disease to luxury succeeds,
And ev'ry death its own avenger breeds;
The fury-passions from that blood began,
And turn'd on man, a fiercer savage, man.

See him from nature rising slow to art!
To copy instinct then was reason's part;
Thus then to man the voice of nature spake,

'Go, from the creatures thy instructions take:
Learn from the birds what food the thickets yield;
Learn from the beasts the physic of the field;
Thy arts of building from the bee receive;
Learn of the mole to plow, the worm to weave;
Learn of the little nautilus to sail,
Spread the thin oar, and catch the driving gale.
Here too all forms of social union find,
And hence let reason, late, instruct mankind:
Here subterranean works and cities see;
There towns aërial on the waving tree.
Learn each small people's genius, policies,
The ant's republic, and the realm of bees;
How those in common all their wealth bestow,
And anarchy without confusion know;
And these forever, tho' a monarch reign,
Their separate cells and properties maintain.
Mark what unvary'd laws preserve each state,
Laws wise as nature, and as fix'd as fate.
In vain thy reason finer webs shall draw,
Entangle justice in her net of law,
And right, too rigid, harden into wrong;
Still for the strong too weak, the weak too strong.
Yet go! and thus o'er all the creatures sway,
Thus let the wiser make the rest obey;
And for those arts mere instinct could afford,
Be crown'd as monarchs, or as gods ador'd.'

V.

Great nature spoke; observant man obey'd;
Cities were built, societies were made:
Here rose one little state; another near
Grew by like means, and join'd, thro' love or fear.
Did here the trees with ruddier burdens bend,
And there the streams in purer rills descend?
What war could ravish, commerce could bestow,
And he return'd a friend, who came a foe.
Converse and love mankind might strongly draw,
When love was liberty, and nature law.
Thus states were form'd; the name of king unknown,
'Till common int'rest plac'd the sway in one.
'Twas virtue only (or in arts or arms,
Diffusing blessings, or averting harms)
The same which in a sire the sons obey'd,
A prince the father of a people made.

VI.

'Till then, by nature crown'd, each patriarch sate,
King, priest and parent of his growing state;
On him, their second providence, they hung,
Their law his eye, their oracle his tongue.
He from the wand'ring furrow call'd the food,
Taught to command the fire, control the flood,
Draw forth the monsters of th' abyss profound,
Or fetch th' aërial eagle to the ground,
'Till drooping, sick'ning, dying, they began
Whom they rever'd as God to mourn as man:
Then, looking up from sire to sire, explor'd
One great first father, and that first ador'd.
Or plain tradition that this All begun,
Convey'd unbroken faith from sire to son;
The worker from the work distinct was known,
And simple reason never sought but one:
Ere wit oblique had broke that steady light,
Man, like his maker, saw that all was right;
To virtue, in the paths of pleasure trod,
And own'd a father when he own'd a God.
Love all the faith, and all th' allegiance then;
For nature knew no right divine in men,
No ill could fear in God; and understood
A sov'reign being, but a sov'reign good.
True faith, true policy, united ran,
That was but love of God, and this of man.

Who first taught souls enslav'd, and realms undone,
Th' enormous faith of many made for one;
That proud exception to all nature's laws,
T'invert the world, and counter-work its cause?
Force first made conquest, and that conquest, law;
'Till superstition taught the tyrant awe,
Then shar'd the tyranny, then lent it aid,
And gods of conqu'rors, slaves of subjects made:
She, 'midst the lightning's blaze, and thunder's sound,
When rock'd the mountains, and when groan'd the ground,
She taught the weak to bend, the proud to pray,
To pow'r unseen, and mightier far than they:
She, from the rending earth, and bursting skies,
Saw gods descend, and fiends infernal rise:
Here fix'd the dreadful, there the blest abodes;
Fear made her devils, and weak hope her gods;
Gods partial, changeful, passionate, unjust,
Whose attributes were rage, revenge, or lust;

Such as the souls of cowards might conceive,
And, form'd like tyrants, tyrants would believe.
Zeal then, not charity, became the guide;
And hell was built on spite, and heav'n on pride.
Then sacred seem'd th' ether'al vault no more;
Altars grew marble then, and reek'd with gore:
Then first the flamen tasted living food;
Next his grim idol smear'd with human blood;
With heav'n's own thunders shook the world below,
And play'd the god an engine on his foe.

So drives self-love, thro' just, and thro' unjust,
To one man's pow'r, ambition, lucre, lust.
The same self-love, in all, becomes the cause
Of what restrains him, government and laws.
For, what one likes, if others like as well,
What serves one will, when many wills rebel?
How shall he keep, what, sleeping or awake,
A weaker may surprise, a stronger take?
His safety must his liberty restrain:
All join to guard what each desires to gain.
Forc'd into virtue thus, by self-defence,
Ev'n kings learn'd justice and benevolence:
Self-love forsook the path it first pursu'd,
And found the private in the public good.

'Twas then the studious head or gen'rous mind,
Follow'r of God, or friend of human-kind,
Poet or patriot, rose but to restore
The faith and moral nature gave before;
Relum'd her ancient light, not kindled new,
If not God's image, yet his shadow drew:
Taught pow'r's due use to people and to kings,
Taught nor to slack, nor strain its tender strings,
The less, or greater, set so justly true,
That touching one must strike the other too;
'Till jarring int'rests, of themselves create
Th' according music of a well-mix'd state.
Such is the world's great harmony, that springs
From order, union, full consent of things:
Where small and great, where weak and mighty, made
To serve, not suffer, strengthen, not invade;
More pow'rful each as needful to the rest,
And in proportion as it blesses, blest;
Draw to one point, and to one centre bring
Beast, man, or angel, servant, lord, or king.

For forms of government let fools contest;

Whate'er is best administer'd is best:
For modes of faith, let graceless zealots fight;
His can't be wrong whose life is in the right:
In faith and hope the world will disagree,
But all mankind's concern is Charity:
All must be false that thwart this one great end;
And all of God, that bless mankind, or mend.

Man, like the gen'rous vine, supported lives;
The strength he gains is from th' embrace he gives.
On their own axis as the planets run,
Yet make at once their circle round the sun;
So two consistent motions act the soul;
And one regards itself, and one the whole.
Thus God and nature link'd the gen'ral frame,
And bade self-love and social be the same.

An Essay on Man

Epistle IV—Of the Nature and State of Man with Respect to Happiness

Oh Happiness! our being's end and aim!
Good, pleasure, ease, content! whate'er thy name:
That something still which prompts th' eternal sigh,
For which we bear to live, or dare to die,
Which still so near us, yet beyond us lies,
O'er-look'd, seen double, by the fool, and wise.
Plant of celestial seed! if dropt below,
Say, in what mortal soil thou deign'st to grow?
Fair op'ning to some court's propitious shine,
Or deep with di'monds in the flaming mine?
Twin'd with the wreaths Parnassian laurels yield,

Or reap'd in iron harvests of the field?
Where grows?—where grows it not? If vain our toil,
We ought to blame the culture, not the soil:
Fix'd to no spot is happiness sincere,
'Tis nowhere to be found, or ev'rywhere:
'Tis never to be bought, but always free,
And fled from monarchs, St. John! dwells with thee.

Ask of the learn'd the way? The learn'd are blind;
This bids to serve, and that to shun mankind;
Some place the bliss in action, some in ease,
Those call it pleasure, and contentment these;
Some sunk to beasts, find pleasure end in pain;

Some swell'd to gods, confess e'en virtue vain;
Or indolent, to each extreme they fall,
To trust in ev'ry thing, or doubt of all.

Who thus define it, say they more or less
Than this, that happiness is happiness?

Take nature's path, and mad opinion's leave;
All states can reach it, and all heads conceive;
Obvious her goods, in no extreme they dwell;
There needs but thinking right, and meaning well;
And mourn our various portions as we please,
Equal is common sense, and common ease.

Remember, man, 'The universal cause
Acts not by partial, but by gen'ral laws';
And makes what happiness we justly call
Subsist not in the good of one, but all.
There's not a blessing individuals find,
But some way leans and hearkens to the kind:
No bandit fierce, no tyrant mad with pride,
No cavern'd hermit, rests self-satisfy'd:
Who most to shun or hate mankind pretend,
Seek an admirer, or who would fix a friend:
Abstract what others feel, what others think,
All pleasures sicken, and all glories sink:
Each has his share; and who would more obtain,
Shall find the pleasure pays not half the pain.

Order is heav'n's first law; and this confest,
Some are, and must be, greater than the rest,
More rich, more wise; but who infers from hence
That such are happier, shocks all common sense.
Heav'n to mankind impartial we confess,
If all are equal in their happiness:
But mutual wants this happiness increase;
All nature's diff'rence keeps all nature's peace.
Condition, circumstance is not the thing;
Bliss is the same in subject or in king,
In who obtain defence, or who defend,
In him who is, or him who finds a friend:
Heav'n breathes thro' ev'ry member of the whole
One common blessing, as one common soul.
But fortune's gifts if each alike possest,
And each were equal, must not all contest?
If then to all men happiness was meant,
God in externals could not place content.

Fortune her gifts may variously dispose,
And these be happy call'd, unhappy those;
But heav'n's just balance equal will appear,
While those are plac'd in hope, and these in fear:
Not present good or ill, the joy or curse,
But future views of better, or of worse.
Oh sons of earth! attempt ye still to rise,
By mountains pil'd on mountains, to the skies?
Heav'n still with laughter the vain toil surveys,
And buries madmen in the heaps they raise.

Know, all the good that individuals find,
Or God and nature meant to mere mankind,
Reason's whole pleasure, all the joys of sense,
Lie in three words, health, peace, and competence
But health consists with temperance alone;
And peace, oh virtue! peace is all thy own.
The good or bad the gifts of fortune gain;
But these less taste them, as they worse obtain.
Say, in pursuit of profit or delight,
Who risk the most, that take wrong means, or right?
Of vice or virtue, whether blest or curst,
Which meets contempt, or which compassion first?
Count all th' advantage prosp'rous vice attains,
'Tis but what virtue flies from and disdains:
And grant the bad what happiness they would,
One they must want, which is, to pass for good.

Oh blind to truth, and God's whole scheme below,
Who fancy bliss to vice, to virtue woe!
Who sees and follows that great scheme the best,
Best knows the blessing, and will most be blest.
But fools the good alone unhappy call,
For ills or accidents that chance to all.
See Falkland dies, the virtuous and the just!
See god-like Turenne prostrate on the dust!
See Sidney bleeds amid the martial strife!
Was this their virtue, or contempt of life?
Say, was it virtue, more tho' heav'n ne'er gave,
Lamented Digby! sunk thee to the grave?
Tell me, if virtue made the son expire,
Why, full of days and honour, lives the sire?
Why drew Marseilles' good bishop purer breath,
When nature sicken'd and each gale was death!
Or why so long (in life if long can be)
Lent heav'n a parent to the poor and me?

What makes all physical or moral ill?

There deviates nature, and here wanders will.
God sends not ill; if rightly understood,
Or partial ill is universal good,
Or change admits, or nature lets it fall,
Short, and but rare, 'till man improv'd it all.
We just as wisely might of heav'n complain
That righteous Abel was destroy'd by Cain,
As that the virtuous son is ill at ease,
When his lewd father gave the dire disease.
Think we, like some weak prince, th' eternal cause
Prone for his fav'rites to reverse his laws?

Shall burning Ætna, if a sage requires,
Forget to thunder, and recall her fires?
On air or sea new motions be imprest,
Oh blameless Bethel! to relieve thy breast?
When the loose mountain trembles from on high
Shall gravitation cease, if you go by?
Or some old temple, nodding to its fall,
For Chartres' head reserve the hanging wall?

But still this world (so fitted for the knave)
Contents us not. A better shall we have?
A kingdom of the just then let it be:
But first consider how those just agree.
The good must merit God's peculiar care;
But who, but God, can tell us who they are?
One thinks on Calvin heav'n's own spirit fell;
Another deems him instrument of hell;
If Calvin feel heav'n's blessing, or its rod,
This cries there is, and that, there is no God.
What shocks one part will edify the rest,
Nor with one system can they all be blest.
The very best will variously incline,
And what rewards your virtue, punish mine.
Whatever is, is right.—This world, 'tis true,
Was made for Cæsar—but for Titus too;
And which more blest, who chain'd his country, say,
Or he whose virtue sigh'd to lose a day?

'But sometimes virtue starves, while vice is fed.'
What then? is the reward of virtue bread?
That vice may merit, 'tis the price of toil;
The knave deserves it, when he tills the soil,
The knave deserves it, when he tempts the main,
Where folly fights for kings, or dives for gain.
The good man may be weak, be indolent;
Nor is his claim to plenty, but content.

But grant him riches, your demand is o'er?
'No, shall the good want health, the good want pow'r?'
Add health and pow'r, and ev'ry earthly thing,
'Why bounded pow'r? why private? why no king?
Nay, why external for internal giv'n?
Why is not man a God, and earth a heav'n?'
Who ask and reason thus, will scarce conceive
God gives enough, while he has more to give:
Immense the pow'r, immense were the demand;
Say, at what part of nature will they stand?

What nothing earthly gives, or can destroy,
The soul's calm sunshine, and the heart-felt joy,
Is virtue's prize: a better would you fix?
Then give humility a coach and six,
Justice a conq'ror's sword, or truth a gown,
Or public spirit its great cure, a crown.
Weak, foolish man! will heav'n reward us there
With the same trash mad mortals wish for here?
The boy and man an individual makes,
Yet sigh'st thou now for apples and for cakes?
Go, like the Indian, in another life
Expect thy dog, thy bottle, and thy wife,
As well as dream such trifles are assign'd,
As toys and empires, for a god-like mind.
Rewards, that either would to virtue bring
No joy, or be destructive of the thing:
How oft by these at sixty are undone
The virtues of a saint at twenty-one!

To whom can riches give repute, or trust,
Content, or pleasure, but the good and just?
Judges and senates have been bought for gold,
Esteem and love were never to be sold.
Oh fool! to think God hates the worthy mind,
The lover and the love of human-kind,
Whose life is healthful, and whose conscience clear,
Because he wants a thousand pounds a year.

Honour and shame from no condition rise;
Act well your part, there all the honour lies.
Fortune in men has some small diff'rence mad'
One flaunts in rags, one flutters in brocade;
The cobler apron'd, and the parson gown'd,
The frier hooded, and the monarch crown'd.
'What differ more (you cry) than crown and cowl?'
I'll tell you, friend! a wise man and a fool.
You'll find, if once the monarch acts the monk,

Or, cobler-like, the parson will be drunk,
Worth makes the man, and want of it, the fellow;
The rest is all but leather or prunella.

Stuck o'er with titles and hung round with strings,
That thou may'st be by kings, or whores of kings.
Boast the pure blood of an illustrious race,
In quiet flow from Lucrece to Lucrece:
But by your fathers' worth if your's you rate,
Count me those only who were good and great.
Go! if your ancient, but ignoble blood
Has crept thro' scoundrels ever since the flood,
Go! and pretend your family is young;
Nor own your fathers have been fools so long.
What can ennoble sots, or slaves, or cowards?
Alas! not all the blood of all the Howards,

Look next on greatness; say where greatness lies.
'Where, but among the heroes and the wise?'
Heroes are much the same, the point's agreed,
From Macedonia's madman to the Swede;
The whole strange purpose of their lives, to find
Or make, an enemy of all mankind!
Not one looks backward, onward still he goes,
Yet ne'er looks forward farther than his nose.
No less alike the politic and wise;
All sly slow things, with circumspective eyes:
Men in their loose unguarded hours they take,
Not that themselves are wise, but others weak.
But grant that those can conquer, these can cheat;
'Tis phrase absurd to call a villain great:
Who wickedly is wise, or madly brave,
Is but the more a fool, the more a knave.
Who noble ends by noble means obtains,
Or failing, smiles in exile or in chains,
Like good Aurelius let him reign, or bleed
Like Socrates, that man is great indeed.

What's fame? a fancy'd life in others' breath,
A thing beyond us, ev'n before our death.
Just what you hear, you have, and what's unknown
The same (my lord) if Tully's, or your own.
All that we feel of it begins and ends
In the small circle of our foes or friends;
To all beside as much an empty shade
An Eugene living, as a Cæsar dead;
Alike or when, or where they shone, or shine,
Or on the Rubicon, or on the Rhine.

A wit's a feather, and a chief a rod;
An honest man's the noblest work of God.
Fame but from death a villain's name can save,
As justice tears his body from the grave;
When what t' oblivion better were resign'd,
Is hung on high, to poison half mankind.
All fame is foreign, but of true desert;
Plays round the head, but comes not to the heart:
One self approving hour whole years out-weighs
Of stupid starers, and of loud huzzas;
And more true joy Marcellus exil'd feels,
Than Cæsar with a senate at his heels.

In parts superior what advantage lies?
Tell (for you can) what is it to be wise?
'Tis but to know how little can be known;
To see all others' faults, and feel your own:
Condemn'd in bus'ness or in arts to drudge,
Without a second, or without a judge:
Truths would you teach, or save a sinking land?
All fear, none aid you, and few understand.
Painful preëminence! yourself to view
Above life's weakness, and its comforts too.

Bring then these blessings to a strict account;
Make fair deductions; see to what they 'mount:
How much of other each is sure to cost;
How each for other oft is wholly lost;
How inconsistent greater goods with these;
How sometimes life is risqu'd, and always ease:
Think, and if still the things thy envy call,
Say, would'st thou be the man to whom they fall?
To sigh for ribbands if thou art so silly,
Mark how they grace Lord Umbra, or Sir Billy.
Is yellow dirt the passion of thy life;
Look but on Gripus, or on Gripus' wife.
If parts allure thee, think how Bacon shin'd,
The wisest, brightest, meanest of mankind:
Or ravish'd with the whistling of a name,
See Cromwell, damn'd to everlasting fame!
If all, united, thy ambition call,
From ancient story learn to scorn them all.
There, in the rich, the honour'd, fam'd and great,
See the false scale of happiness complete!
In hearts of kings, or arms of queens who lay,
How happy those to ruin, these betray.
Mark by what wretched steps their glory grows,
From dirt and sea-weed as proud Venice rose;

In each how guilt and greatness equal ran,
And all that rais'd the hero, sunk the man:
Now Europe's laurels on their brows behold,
But stain'd with blood, or ill-exchang'd for gold:
Then see them broke with toils, or sunk in ease,
Or infamous for plunder'd provinces.
Oh, wealth ill-fated! which no act of fame
E'er taught to shine, or sanctify'd from shame!
What greater bliss attends their close of life?
Some greedy minion, or imperious wife,
The trophy'd arches, story'd halls invade,
And haunt their slumbers in the pompous shade.
Alas! not dazzled with their noon-tide ray,
Compute the morn and ev'ning to the day;
The whole amount of that enormous fame,
A tale, that blends their glory with their shame!

Know then this truth, enough for man to know,
'Virtue alone is happiness below.'
The only point where human bliss stands still,
And tastes the good without the fall to ill;
Where only merit constant pay receives,
Is blest in what it takes, and what it gives;
The joy unequal'd, if its end it gain,
And if it lose, attended with no pain:
Without satiety, tho' e'er so bless'd,
And but more relish'd as the more distress'd:
The broadest mirth unfeeling folly wears,
Less pleasing far than virtue's very tears;
Good, from each object, from each place acquir'd,
For ever exercis'd, yet never tir'd;
Never elated, while one man's oppress'd;
Never dejected, while another's bless'd;
And where no wants, no wishes can remain,
Since but to wish more virtue, is to gain.

See the sole bliss heav'n could on all bestow!
Which who but feels can taste, but thinks can know:
Yet poor with fortune, and with learning blind,
The bad must miss, the good, untaught, will find;
Slave to no sect, who takes no private road,
But looks through nature up to nature's God:
Pursues that chain which links th' immense design,
Joins heav'n and earth, and mortal and divine;
Sees, that no being any bliss can know,
But touches some above, and some below;
Learns, from this union of the rising whole,
The first, last purpose of the human soul;

And knows where faith, law, morals, all began,
All end, in love of God, and love of man.

For him alone, hope leads from goal to goal,
And opens still, and opens on his soul;
'Till lengthen'd on to faith, and unconfin'd,
It pours the bliss that fills up all the mind.
He sees, why nature plants in man alone
Hope of known bliss, and faith in bliss unknown:
(Nature, whose dictates to no other kind
Are giv'n in vain, but what they seek they find)
Wise is her present; she connects in this
His greatest virtue with his greatest bliss;
At once his own bright prospect to be blest,
And strongest motive to assist the rest.

Self-love thus push'd to social, to divine,
Gives thee to make thy neighbour's blessing thine.
Is this too little for the boundless heart?
Extend it, let thy enemies have part:
Grasp the whole worlds of reason, life, and sense,
In one close system of benevolence:
Happier as kinder, in whate'er degree,
And height of bliss but height of charity.

God loves from whole to parts: but human soul
Must rise from individual to the whole.
Self-love but serves the virtuous mind to wake
As the small pebble stirs the peaceful lake;
The centre mov'd, a circle strait succeeds,
Another still, and still another spreads;
Friend, parent, neighbour, first it will embrace;
His country next; and next all human race;
Wide and more wide, th' o'erflowings of the mind
Take ev'ry creature in, of ev'ry kind;
Earth smiles around, with boundless bounty blest,
And heav'n beholds its image in his breast.

Come then, my friend, my genius, come along;
Oh master of the poet, and the song!
And while the muse now stoops, or now ascends,
To man's low passions, or their glorious ends,
Teach me, like thee, in various nature wise,
To fall with dignity, with temper rise;
Form'd by thy converse, happily to steer
From grave to gay, from lively to severe;
Correct with spirit, eloquent with ease,
Intent to reason, or polite to please.

Oh! while along the stream of time thy name
Expanded flies, and gathers all its fame;
Say, shall my little bark attendant sail,
Pursue the triumph, and partake the gale?
When statesmen, heroes, kings, in dust repose,
Whose sons shall blush their fathers were thy foes,
Shall then this verse to future age pretend
Thou wert my guide, philosopher, and friend?
That, urg'd by thee, I turn'd the tuneful art
From sounds to things, from fancy to the heart;
For wit's false mirror held up nature's light;
Shew'd erring pride, whatever is, is right;
That reason, passion, answer one great aim;
That true self-love and social are the same;
That virtue only makes our bliss below;
And all our knowledge is, ourselves to know.

Alexander Pope – A Short Biography

Alexander Pope was born in Lombard Street, London, on the 21st of May 1688—the year of the Revolution. His father was a linen-merchant, in thriving circumstances, and said to have noble blood in his veins. His mother was Edith or Editha Turner, daughter of William Turner, Esq., of York. Mr Carruthers, in his excellent Life of the Poet, mentions that there was an Alexander Pope, a clergyman, in the remote parish of Reay, in Caithness, who rode all the way to Twickenham to pay his great namesake a visit, and was presented by him with a copy of the subscription edition of the "Odyssey," in five volumes quarto, which is still preserved by his descendants. Pope's father had made about £10,000 by trade; but being a Roman Catholic, and fond of a country life, he retired from business shortly after the Revolution, at the early age of forty-six. He resided first at Kensington, and then in Binfield, in the neighbourhood of Windsor Forest. He is said to have put his money in a strong box, and to have lived on the principal. His great delight was in his garden; and both he and his wife seem to have cherished the warmest interest in their son, who was very delicate in health, and their only child. Pope's study is still preserved in Binfield; and on the lawn, a cypress-tree which he is said to have planted, is pointed out.

Pope was a premature and precocious child. His figure was deformed—his back humped—his stature short (four feet six inches)—his legs and arms disproportionably long. He was sometimes compared to a spider, and sometimes to a windmill. The only mark of genius lay in his bright and piercing eye. He was sickly in constitution, and required and received great tenderness and care. Once, when three years old, he narrowly escaped from an angry cow, but was wounded in the throat. He was remarkable as a child for his amiable temper; and from the sweetness of his voice, received the name of the Little Nightingale. His aunt gave him his first lessons in reading, and he soon became an enthusiastic lover of books; and by copying printed characters, taught himself to write. When eight years old, he was placed under the care of the family priest, one Bannister, who taught him the Latin and Greek grammars together. He was next removed to a Catholic seminary at Twyford, near Winchester; and while there, read Ogilby's "Homer" and Sandys's "Ovid" with great delight. He had not been long at this school till he wrote a severe lampoon, of two hundred lines' length, on his master—so truly was the "boy the father of the man"—for which demi-Dunciad he was severely flogged. His father, offended at this, removed him to a London school, kept by a Mr Deane. This man taught the poet nothing; but his residence in London gave him the opportunity of attending the theatres. With these he was so captivated, that he wrote a kind of play, which was acted by his schoolfellows, consisting of speeches from Ogilby's "Iliad," tacked together with verses of his own. He became acquainted with Dryden's works, and went to Wills's coffee-house to see him. He says, "Virgilium tantum vidi." Such transient meetings of literary orbs are among the most interesting passages in biography. Thus met Galileo with Milton, Milton with Dryden, Dryden with Pope, and Burns with Scott. Carruthers strikingly remarks, "Considering the perils and uncertainties of a literary life—its precarious rewards, feverish anxieties, mortifications, and disappointments, joined to the tyranny of the Tonsons and Lintots, and the malice and envy of dunces, all of which Dryden had long and bitterly experienced—the aged poet could hardly have looked at the delicate and deformed boy, whose preternatural acuteness and sensibility were seen in his dark eyes, without a feeling approaching to grief, had he known that he was to fight a battle like that under which he was himself then sinking, even though the Temple of Fame should at length open to receive him." At twelve, he wrote the "Ode to Solitude;" and shortly after, his satirical piece on Elkanah Settle, and some of his translations and imitations. His next period, he says, was in Windsor Forest, where for several years he did nothing but read the classics and indite poetry. He wrote a tragedy, a comedy, and four books of an Epic called "Alexander," all of which afterwards he committed to the flames. He translated also a portion of Statius, and Cicero "De Senectute," and "thought himself the greatest genius that ever was." His father encouraged him in his studies, and when his verses did not please him, sent him back to "new turn" them, saying, "These are not good rhymes." His principal favourites were Virgil's "Eclogues," in Latin; and in English, Spencer, Waller, and Dryden—admiring Spencer, we presume, for his luxuriant fancy, Waller for his smooth versification, and Dryden for his vigorous sense and vivid sarcasm. In the Forest, he became acquainted with Sir William Trumbull, the retired secretary of state, a man of general accomplishments, who read, rode, conversed with the youthful poet; introduced him to old Wycherley, the dramatist; and was of material service to his views. With Wycherley, who was old, doted, and excessively vain, Pope did not continue long intimate. A coldness, springing from some criticisms which the youth ventured to make on the veteran's poetry, crept in between them. Walsh of Abberley, in Worcestershire, a man of good sense and taste, became, after a perusal of the "Pastorals" in MS., a warm friend and kind adviser of Pope's, who has immortalised him in more than one of his poems. Walsh told Pope that there had never hitherto appeared in Britain a poet who was at once great and correct, and exhorted him to aim at accuracy and elegance.

When fifteen, he visited London, in order to acquire a more thorough knowledge of French and Italian. At sixteen, he wrote the "Pastorals," and a portion of "Windsor Forest," although they were not published for some time afterwards. By his incessant exertions, he now began to feel his constitution injured. He imagined himself dying, and sent farewell letters to all his friends, including the Abbé Southcot. This gentleman communicated Pope's case to Dr Ratcliffe, who gave him some medical directions; by following which, the poet recovered. He was advised to relax in his studies, and to ride daily; and he prudently followed the advice. Many years afterwards, he repaid the benevolent Abbé by procuring for him, through Sir Robert Walpole, the nomination to an abbey in Avignon. This is only one of many proofs that, notwithstanding his waspish temper, and his no small share of malice as well as vanity, there was a warm heart in our poet.

In 1707, Pope became acquainted with Michael Blount of Maple, Durham, near Reading; whose two sisters, Martha and Teresa, he has commemorated in various verses. On his connexion with these ladies, some mystery rests. Bowles has strongly and plausibly urged that it was not of the purest or most creditable order. Others have contended that it did not go further than the manners of the age sanctioned; and they say, "a much greater license in conversation and in epistolary correspondence was permitted between the sexes than in our decorous age!" We are not careful to try and settle such a delicate question—only we are inclined to suspect, that when common decency quits the words of male and female parties in their mutual communications, it is a very ample charity that can suppose it to adhere to their actions. And nowhere do we find grosser language than in some of Pope's prose epistles to the Blounts.

His "Pastorals," after having been handed about in MS., and shewn to such reputed judges as Lord Halifax, Lord Somers, Garth, Congreve, &c., were at last, in 1709, printed in the sixth volume of Tonson's "Miscellanies." Like all well-finished commonplaces, they were received with instant and universal applause. It is humiliating to contrast the reception of these empty echoes of inspiration, these agreeable centos, with that of such genuine, although faulty poems, as Keat's "Endymion," Shelley's "Queen Mab," and Wordsworth's "Lyrical Ballads." Two years later, (in 1711), a far better and more characteristic production from his pen was ushered anonymously into the world. This was the "Essay on Criticism," a work which he had first written in prose, and which discovers a ripeness of judgment, a clearness of thought, a condensation of style, and a command over the information he possesses, worthy of any age in life, and almost of any mind in time. It serves, indeed, to shew what Pope's true forte was. That lay not so much in poetry, as in the knowledge of its principles and laws, not so much in creation, as in criticism. He was no Homer or Shakspeare; but he might have been nearly as acute a judge of poetry as Aristotle, and nearly as eloquent an expounder of the rules of art and the glories of genius as Longinus.

In the same year, Pope printed "The Rape of the Lock," in a volume of Miscellanies. Lord Petre had, much in the way described by the poet, stolen a lock of Miss Belle Fermor's hair, a feat which led to an estrangement between the families. Pope set himself to reconcile them by this beautiful poem, a poem which has embalmed at once the quarrel and the reconciliation to all future time. In its first version, the machinery was awanting, the "lock" was a desert, the "rape" a natural event, the small infantry of sylphs and gnomes were slumbering uncreated in the poet's mind; but in the next edition he contrived to introduce them in a manner so easy and so exquisite, as to remind you of the variations which occur in dreams, where one wonder seems softly to slide into the bosom of another, and where beautiful and fantastic fancies grow suddenly out of realities, like the bud from the bough, or the fairy-seeming wing of the summer-cloud from the stern azure of the heavens.

A little after this, Pope became acquainted with a far greater, better, and truer man than himself, Joseph Addison. Warburton, and others, have sadly misrepresented the connexion between these two famous wits, as well as their relative intellectual positions. Addison was a more amiable and childlike person than Pope. He had much more, too, of the Christian. He was not so elaborately polished and furbished as the author of "The Rape of the Lock;" but he had, naturally, a finer and richer genius. Pope found early occasion for imagining Addison his disguised enemy. He gave him a hint of his intention to introduce the machinery into "The Rape of the Lock." Of this, Addison disapproved, and said it was a delicious little thing already—merum sal. This, Pope, and some of his friends, have attributed to jealousy; but it is obvious that Addison could not foresee the success with which the machinery was to be managed, and did foresee the difficulties connected with tinkering such an exquisite production. We may allude here to the circumstances which, at a later date, produced an estrangement between these celebrated men. When Tickell, Addison's friend, published the first book of the "Iliad," in opposition to Pope's version, Addison gave it the preference. This moved Pope's indignation, and led him to assert that it was Addison's own composition. In this conjecture he was supported by Edward Young, who had known Tickell long and intimately, and had never heard of him having written at college, as was averred, this translation. It is now, however, we believe, certain, from the MS. which still exists, that Tickell was the real author. A coldness, from this date, began between Pope and Addison. An attempt to reconcile them only made matters worse; and at last the breach was rendered irremediable by Pope's writing the famous character of his rival, afterwards inserted in the Prologue to the Satires, a portrait drawn with the perfection of polished malice and bitter sarcasm, but which seems more a caricature than a likeness. Whatever Addison's faults, his conduct to Pope did not deserve such a return. The whole passage is only one of those painful incidents which disgrace the history of letters, and prove how much spleen, ingratitude, and baseness often co-exist with the highest parts. The words of Pope are as true now as ever they were—"the life of a wit is a warfare upon earth;" and a warfare in which poisoned missiles and every variety of falsehood are still common. We may also here mention, that while the friendship of Pope and Addison lasted, the former contributed the well-known prologue to the latter's "Cato."

One of Pope's most intimate friends in his early days was Henry Cromwell—a distant relative of the great Oliver—a gentleman of fortune, gallantry, and literary taste, who became his agreeable and fascinating, but somewhat dangerous, companion. He is supposed to have initiated Pope into some of the fashionable follies of the town. At this time, Pope's popularity roused one of his most formidable foes against him. This was that Cobbett of criticism, old John Dennis, a man of strong natural powers, much learning, and a rich, coarse vein of humour; but irascible, vindictive, vain, and capricious. Pope had provoked him by an attack in his "Essay on Criticism," and the savage old man revenged himself by a running fire of fierce diatribes against that "Essay" and "The Rape of the Lock." Pope waited till Dennis had committed himself by a powerful but furious assault on Addison's "Cato" (most of which Johnson has preserved in his Life of Pope); and then, partly to court Addison, and partly to indulge his spleen at the critic, wrote a prose satire, entitled, "The Narrative of Dr Robert Norris on the Frenzy of J.D." In this, however, he overshot the mark; and Addison signified to him that he was displeased with the spirit of his narrative, an intimation which Pope keenly resented. This scornful dog would not eat the dirty pudding that was graciously flung to him; and Pope found that, without having conciliated Addison, he had made Dennis's furnace of hate against himself seven times hotter than before.

In 1712 appeared "The Messiah," "The Dying Christian to his Soul," "The Temple of Fame," and the "Elegy on the Memory of an Unfortunate Lady." Her story is still involved in mystery. Her name is said to have been Wainsbury. She was attached to a lover above her degree, some say to the Duke of Berry, whom she had met in her early youth in France. In despair of obtaining her desire, she hanged herself. It is curious, if true, that she was as deformed in person as Pope himself. Her family seems to have been noble. In 1713, he published "Windsor Forest," an "Ode on St Cecilia's Day," and several papers in the Guardian—one of them being an exquisitely ironical paper, comparing Phillip's pastorals with his own, and affecting to give them the preference—the extracts being so selected as to damage his rival's claims. This year, also, he wrote, although he did not publish, his fine epistle to Jervas, the painter. Pope was passionately fond of the art of painting, and practised it a good deal under Jervas's instructions, although he did not reach great proficiency. The prodigy has yet to be born who combines the characters of a great painter and a great poet.

About this time, Pope commenced preparations for the great work of translating Homer; and subscription-papers, accordingly, were issued. Dean Swift was now in England, and took a deep interest in the success of this undertaking, recommending it in coffee-houses, and introducing the subject and Pope's name to the leading Tories. Pope met the Dean for the first time in Berkshire, where, in one of his fits of savage disgust at the conflicting parties of the period, he had retired to the house of a clergyman, and an intimacy commenced which was only terminated by death. We have often regretted that Pope had not selected some author more suitable to his genius than Homer. Horace or Lucretius, or even Ovid, would have been more congenial. His imitations of Horace shew us what he might have made of a complete translation. What a brilliant thing a version of Lucretius, in the style of the "Essay on Man," would have been! And his "Rape of the Lock" proves that he had considerable sympathy with the elaborate fancy, although not with the meretricious graces of Ovid. But with Homer, the severely grand, the simple, the warlike, the lover and painter of all Nature's old original forms—the ocean, the mountains, and the stars—what thorough sympathy could a man have who never saw a real mountain or a battle, and whose enthusiasm for scenery was confined to purling brooks, trim gardens, artificial grottos, and the shades of Windsor Forest? Accordingly, his Homer, although a beautiful and sparkling poem, is not a satisfactory translation of the "Iliad," and still less of the "Odyssey." He has trailed along the naked lances of the Homeric lines so many flowers and leaves that you can hardly recognise them, and feel that their point is deadened and their power gone. This at least is our opinion; although many to this day continue to admire these translations, and have even said that if they are not Homer, they are something better.

The "Iliad" took him six years, and was a work which cost him much anxiety as well as labour, the more as his scholarship was far from profound. He was assisted in the undertaking by Parnell (who wrote the Life of Homer), by Broome, Jortin, and others. The first volume appeared in June 1715, and the other volumes followed at irregular intervals. He began it in 1712, his twenty-fifth year, and finished it in 1718, his thirtieth year. Previous to its appearance, his remuneration for his poems had been small, and his circumstances were embarrassed; but the result of the subscription, which amounted to £5320, 4s., rendered him independent for life.

While at Binfield, he had often visited London; and there, in the society of Howe, Garth, Parnell, and the rest, used to indulge in occasional excesses, which did his feeble constitution no good; and once, according to Colley Cibber, he narrowly escaped a serious scrape in a house of a certain description, Colley, by his own account, "helping out the tomtit for the sake of Homer!" This statement, indeed, Pope has denied; but his veracity was by no means his strongest point. After writing a "Farewell to London," he retired, in 1715, to Twickenham, along with his parents; and remained there, cultivating his garden, digging his grottos, and diversifying his walks, till the end of his days.

Some years before, he had become acquainted with Lady Mary Wortley Montague, the most brilliant woman of her age—witty, fascinating, beautiful, and accomplished—full of enterprise and spirit, too, although decidedly French in her tastes, manners, and character. Pope fell violently in love with her, and had her undoubtedly in his eye when writing "Eloisa and Abelard," which he did at Oxford in 1716, shortly after her going abroad, and which appeared the next year. His passion was not requited, nay, was treated with contempt and ridicule; and he became in after years a bitter enemy and foul-mouthed detractor of the lady, although after her return, in 1718, she resided near him at Twickenham, and they seemed outwardly on good terms.

In 1717, and the succeeding year, Pope lost successively his father, Parnell, Garth, and Rowe, and bitterly felt their loss. He finished, as we have seen, the "Iliad" in 1718; but the fifth and sixth volumes, which were the last, did not appear till 1720. Its success, which at the time was triumphant, roused against him the whole host of envy and detraction. Dennis, and all Grub Street with him, were moved to assail him. Pamphlets after pamphlets were published, all of which, after reading with writhing anguish, Pope had the resolution to bind up into volumes—a great collection of calumny, which he preserved, probably, for purposes of future revenge. His own friends, on the other hand, hailed his work with applause, Gay writing a most graceful and elegant poem, in ottava rima, entitled, "Mr Pope's Welcome Home from Greece," in which his different friends are pictured as receiving him home on the shores of Britain, after an absence of six years. Bentley, that stern old Grecian, avoided the extremes of a howling

Grub Street on the one hand, and a flattering aristocracy on the other, and expressed what is, we think, the just opinion when he said, "It is a pretty poem, but it is not Homer."

In 1721, he issued a selection from the poems of Parnell, and prefixed a very beautiful dedication to the Earl of Oxford, commencing with—

"Such were the notes thy once-loved poet sung,
Till death untimely stopp'd his tuneful tongue.
Oh, just beheld and lost, admired and mourn'd,
With softest manners, gentlest arts adorn'd!"

In 1722, he engaged to translate the "Odyssey." He employed Broome and Fenton as his assistants in the work; and the portions translated by them were thought as good as his. He remunerated them very handsomely. Of this work, the first three quarto volumes appeared in 1725; and the fourth and fifth, which completed the work, the following year. Pope sold the copyright to Lintot for £600.

He was busy at this time, too, with an edition of Shakspeare, not quite worthy of either poet. It appeared in six volumes, quarto, in 1725. His preface was good, but he was deficient in antiquarian lore; and his mortification was extreme when Theobald, destined to figure in "The Dunciad," a mere plodding hack, not only in his "Shakspeare Restored," exposed many blunders in Pope's edition; but issued, some years afterwards, an edition of his own, which was much better received by the public.

In 1726, there was a great gathering of the Tory wits at Twickenham. Swift had come from Ireland, and resided for some time with Pope. Bolingbroke came over occasionally from Dawley; and Gay was often there to laugh with, and be laughed at by, the rest. Swift had "Gulliver's Travels"—the most ingenious and elaborate libel against man and God ever written—in his pocket, nearly ready for publication; and we may conceive the grim, sardonic smile with which he read it to his friends, and their tumultuous mirth. Gay was projecting his "Beggars' Opera," and Pope preparing some of his witty "Miscellanies." At the end of two months, the Dean was hurried home by the tidings of Stella's illness. He left the "Travels" behind him, for the copyright of which Pope procured £300, a sum counted then very large, and which Swift generously handed over to Pope.

In September this year, when returning in Lord Bolingbroke's coach from Dawley, the poet was overturned in a little rivulet near Twickenhan, and nearly drowned. The unfortunate little man! One is reminded of Gulliver's accident in the Brobdignagian cream-pot. In trying to break the glasses of the coach, which were down, he severely cut his right hand, and lost the use of two of his fingers, an addition to his other deformities not very desirable; and we suspect that Pope thought Voltaire (who had met him at Bolingbroke's) but a miserable comforter, when, in a letter of pretended condolence, he asked—"Is it possible that those fingers which have written 'The Rape of the Lock,' and dressed Homer so becomingly in an English coat, should have been so barbarously treated? Let the hand of Dennis or of your poetasters be cut off; yours is sacred." It was perhaps in keeping that those mutilated fingers were soon to be employed in attacking Dennis, and that the embittered poet was about, with the half of his hand, but with the whole of his heart, to write "The Dunciad."

In the end of April 1727, we find Swift again in Twickenham, where his irritation at the continued ascendancy of Sir Robert Walpole served to infuse more venom into the "Miscellanies" concocted between him and Pope, two volumes of which appeared in June this year. Gay, also, and the ingenious and admirable Dr Arbuthnot, contributed their quota to these volumes. Swift speedily fell ill with that giddiness and deafness which were the avant-couriers of his final malady; and in August he left Twickenham, and in October, London and England, for ever.

In these "Miscellanies" there appeared the famous "Memoirs of Martinus Scriblerus," written chiefly by Pope, in which he lashed the various proficients in the bathos, under the names of flying fishes, swallows, parrots, frogs, eels, &c., and appended the initials of well-known authors to each head. This roused Grub Street, whose malice had nearly fallen asleep, into fresh fury, and he was bitterly assailed in every possible form. Like Hyder Ali, he now—to travesty Burke—"in the recesses of a mind capacious of such things, determined to leave all Duncedom an everlasting monument of vengeance, and became at length so confident of his force, so collected in his might, that he made no secret whatever of his dreadful resolution, but, compounding all the materials of fun, sarcasm, irony, and invective, into one black cloud, he hung for a while on the declivities of Richmond Hill; and whilst the authors were idly and stupidly gazing on this menacing meteor which blackened all their horizon, it suddenly burst and poured down the whole of its contents on the garrets of Grub Street. Then issued a scene of (ludicrous) woe, the like of which no eye had seen, no heart conceived, and which no tongue can adequately tell. All the horrors of literary war before known or heard of—(MacFlecknoe, the Rehearsal, &c.)—were mercy to the new tempest of havoc which burst from the brain of this remorseless poet. A storm of universal laughter filled every bookseller's shop, and penetrated into the remotest attics. The miserable dunces, in part, were stricken mad with rage—in part, dumb with consternation. Some fled for refuge to ale, and others to ink; while not a few fell, or feared to fall, into the 'jaws of famine.'" This singular poem was written in 1727. It was first printed surreptitiously (i.e., with the connivance of the author) in Dublin, and then reprinted in London. The first perfect edition, however, did not appear in London till 1729. On the day of its publication, according to Pope, a crowd of authors besieged the publisher's shop; and by entreaties, threats, nay, cries of treason, tried to hinder its appearance. What a scene it must have been—of teeth gnashing above ragged coats, and eyes glaring through old periwigs—of faces livid with famine and ferocity; while, to complete the confusion, hawkers, booksellers, and even lords, were mixed with the crowd, clamouring for its issue! And as, says Pope, "there is no stopping a torrent with a finger, out it came." The consequence he had foreseen. A universal howl of rage and pain burst from the aggrieved dunces, on whose naked sides the hot pitch had fallen. They pushed their rejoinders beyond the limits of civilised literary warfare; and although Pope had been coarse in his language, they were coarser far, and their blackguardism was not redeemed by wit or genius. Pope felt, or seemed to feel, entire indifference as to these assaults. On some of them, indeed, he could afford to look down with contempt, on account of their obvious animus and gross language. Others, again, were neutralised by the fact, that their authors had provoked reprisals by their previous insults or ingratitude to Pope. Many, however, were too obscure for his notice; and some, such as Aaron Hill and Bentley, did not deserve to be classed with the Theobalds and Ralphs. To Hill, he, after some finessing, was compelled to make an apology. Altogether, although this production increased Pope's fame, and the conception of his power, it did not tend to shew him in the most amiable light, or perhaps to promote his own comfort or peace of mind. After having emptied out his bile in "The Dunciad," he ought to have become mellower in temper, and resigned satire for ever. He continued, on the contrary, as ill-natured as before; and although he afterwards flew at higher game, the iron had entered into his soul, and he remained a satirist, and therefore an unhappy man, for life.

In 1731 appeared an "Epistle on Taste," which was very favourably received; only his enemies accused him of having satirised the Duke of Chandos in it, a man who had befriended Pope, and had lent him money. Pope denied the charge, although it is very possible, both from his own temperament, and from the frequent occurrence of similar cases of baseness in literary life, that it may have been true. Nothing is more common than for those who have been most liberally helped, to become first the secret, and then the open, enemies of their benefactors. In 1732 appeared his epistle on "The Use of Riches," addressed to Lord Bathurst. These two epistles were afterwards incorporated in his "Moral Essays."

As far back as 1725, Pope had been revolving the subject of the "Essay on Man;" and, indeed, some of its couplets remind you of "pebbles which had long been rolled over and polished in the ocean of his mind." It has been asserted, but not proved, that Lord Bolingbroke gave him the outline of this essay in prose. It is unquestionable, indeed, that Bolingbroke exercised influence over Pope's mind, and may have suggested some of the thoughts in the Essay; but it is not probable that a man like Pope would have set himself on such a subject simply to translate from another's mind. He published the first epistle of the Essay, in 1732, anonymously, as an experiment, and had the satisfaction to see it successful. It was received with rapture, and passed through several editions ere the author was known; although we must say that the value of this reception is considerably lessened, when we remember that the critics could not have been very acute who did not detect Pope's "fine Roman hand" in every sentence of this brilliant but most unsatisfactory and shallow performance.

In the same year died dear, simple-minded Gay, who found in Pope a sincere mourner, and an elegant elegiast; and on the 7th of June 1733, expired good old Mrs Pope, at the age of ninety-four. Pope, who had always been a dutiful son, erected an obelisk in his own grounds to her memory, with a simple but striking inscription in Latin. During this year, he published the third part of the "Essay on Man," an epistle to Lord Cobham, On the Knowledge and Characters of Man, and an Imitation of the First Satire of the Second Book of Horace. In this last, he attacks, in the most brutal style, his former love Lady Mary W. Montague, who replied in a piece of coarse cleverness, entitled, "Verses to the Imitator of the First Satire of the Second Book of Horace,"—verses in which she was assisted by Lord Harvey, another of Pope's victims. He wrote, but was prudent enough to suppress, an ironical reply.

In 1734 appeared his very clever and highly-finished epistle to Dr Arbuthnot (now entitled the "Prologue to the Satires"), who was then languishing toward death. Arbuthnot, from his deathbed, solemnly advised Pope to regulate his satire, and seems to have been afraid of his personal safety from his numerous foes. Pope replied in a manly but self-defensive style. He is said about this time to have in his walks carried arms, and had a large dog as his protector; but none of the dunces had courage enough to assail him. Dennis, who was no dunce, might have ventured on it—but he had become miserably infirm, poor, and blind; and Pope had heaped coals of fire on his head, by contributing a Prologue to a play which was acted for his behoof.

Our author's life becomes now little else than a record of multiplying labours and increasing infirmities. In 1734 appeared the fourth part of the "Essay on Man," and the Second Satire of the Second Book of Horace. In 1735 were issued his "Characters of Women: An Epistle to a Lady" (Martha Blount). In this appears his famous character of Atossa—the Duchess of Marlborough. It is said—we fear too truly—that these lines being shewn to her Grace, as a character of the Duchess of Buckingham, she recognised in them her own likeness, and bribed Pope with a thousand pounds to suppress it. He did so religiously—as long as she was alive—and then published it! In the same year he printed a second volume of his "Miscellaneous Works," in folio and quarto, uniform with the "Iliad" and "Odyssey," including a versification of the Satires of Donne; also, anonymously, a production disgraceful to his memory, entitled, "Sober Advice from Horace to the Young Gentlemen about Town," in which he commits many gross indecorums of language, and annexes the name of the great Bentley to several indecent notes. It is said that Bentley, when he read the pamphlet, cried, "'Tis an impudent dog, but I talked against his Homer, and the portentous cub never forgives."

The "Essay on Man" and the "Moral Epistles" were designed to be parts of a great system of ethics, which Pope had long revolved in his mind, and wished to incarnate in poetry. At this time occurred the strange, mysterious circumstances connected with the publication of his letters. It seems that, in 1729, Pope had recalled from his correspondents the letters he had written them, of many of which he had kept no copies. He was induced to this by the fact, that after Henry Cromwell's death, his mistress, Mrs Thomas, who was in indigent circumstances, had sold the letters which had passed between Pope and her keeper, to Curll the bookseller, who had published them without scruple. When Pope obtained his correspondence, he, according to his own statement, burned a great many and laid past the others, after having had a copy of them taken, and deposited in Lord Oxford's library. And his charge against Curll was, that he obtained surreptitiously some of these letters, and published them without Pope's consent. But, ere we come to the circumstances of the publication, several other things require to be noticed. In 1733, Curll, anxious to publish a Life of Pope, advertised for information; and, in consequence, one P.T., who professed to be an old friend of Pope's and his father's, wrote Curll a letter, giving an account of Pope's ancestry, which tallied exactly with what Pope himself, in a note to one of his poems, furnished the following year. P.T., in a second letter, offered to the publisher a large collection of Pope's letters, and inclosed a copy of an advertisement he had drawn out to be published by Curll. Strange as it seems, Curll took no notice of the proposal till 1735, when, having accidentally turned up a copy of P.T.'s advertisement, he sent it to Pope, with a letter requesting an interview, and mentioning that he had some papers of P.T.'s in reference to his family history, which he would shew him. Pope replied by three advertisements in the papers, denying all knowledge of P.T. or his collection of letters or MSS. P.T. then wrote Curll that he had printed the letters at his own expense, seeking a sum of money for them, and appointing an interview at a tavern to shew him the sheets. This was countermanded the next day, P.T. professing to be afraid of Pope and his "bravoes," although how Pope was to know of this meeting was, according to Curll, "the cream of the jest."

Soon after, a round, fat man, with a clergyman's gown and a barrister's band, called on Curll, at ten o'clock at night. He said his name was Smith, that he was a cousin of P.T.'s, and shewed the book in sheets, along with about a dozen of the original letters. After a good deal of negotiation with this personage, Curll obtained fifty copies of P.T.'s printed copies, and issued a flaming advertisement announcing the publication of Pope's letters for thirty years, and stating that the original MSS. were lying at his shop, and might be seen by any who chose, although not a single MS. seems to have been delivered. Smith, the day that the advertisement appeared, handed over, for a sum of money, about three hundred volumes to Curll. But as in the advertisement it was stated that various letters of lords were included, and as there is a law amongst regulations of the Upper House that no peer's letters can be published without his consent, at the instance of the Earl of Jersey, and in consequence, too, of an advertisement of Pope's, the books were seized, and Curll, and the printer of the paper where the advertisement appeared, were ordered to appear at the bar for breach of privilege. P.T. wrote Curll to tell him to conceal all that passed between him and the publisher, and promising him more valuable letters still. Curll, however, told the whole story; and as, when the books were examined, not a single lord's letter was found among them, Curll was acquitted, his books restored to him, the lords saying that they had been made the tools of Pope; and he proceeded to advertise the correspondence, in terms most insulting to Pope, who now felt himself compelled (!) to print, by subscription, his genuine letters, which, when printed, turned out, strange to tell, to be identical with those published by the rapacious bookseller! On viewing the whole transaction, we incline with Johnson, Warton, Bowles, Macaulay, and Carruthers, to look upon it as one of Pope's ape-like stratagems—to believe that P.T. was himself, Smith his agent, and that his objects were partly to outwit Curll, to mystify the public, to gratify that strange love of manoeuvring which dwelt as strongly in him as in any match-making mamma, and to attract interest and attention to the genuine correspondence when it should appear. Pope, it was said, could not "drink tea without a stratagem," and far less publish his correspondence without a series of contemptible tricks—tricks, however, in which he was true to his nature—that being a curious compound of the woman and the wit, the monkey and the genius.

In 1737, four of his Imitations of Horace were published, and in the next year appeared two Dialogues, each entitled "1738," which now form the Epilogue to the Satires. One of them was issued on the same day with Johnson's "London." In that year, too, he published his "Universal Prayer,"—a singular specimen of latitudinarian thought, expressed in a loose simplicity of language, quite unusual with its author. The next year he had intended to signalise by a third Dialogue, which he commenced in a vigorous style, but which he did not finish, owing to the dread of a prosecution before the Lords; and with the exception of letters (one of them interesting, as his last to Swift), his pen was altogether idle. In 1740, he did nothing but edit an edition of select Italian Poets. This year, Crousaz, a Swiss professor of note, having attacked (we think most justly) the "Essay on Man" as a mere Pagan prolusion—a thin philosophical smile cast on the Gordian knot of the mystery of the universe, instead of a sword cutting, or trying to cut, it in sunder—Warburton, a man of much talent and learning, but of more astuteness and anxiety to exalt himself, came forward to the rescue, and, with a mixture of casuistical cunning and real ingenuity, tried, as some one has it, "to make Pope a Christian," although, even in Warburton's hands, like the dying Donald Bane in "Waverley," he "makes but a queer Christian after all;" and his system, essentially Pantheistic, contrives to ignore the grand Scripture principles of a Fall, of a Divine Redeemer, of a Future World, and the glorious light or darkness which these and other Christian doctrines cast upon the Mystery of Man. If, however, Warburton, with all his scholastic subtlety, failed to make Pope a Christian, he made him a warm friend; Allen, Pope's acquaintance, a rich father-in-law; and himself, by and by, the Bishop of Gloucester. Sophistry has seldom, although sometimes, been thus richly rewarded.

The last scene of Pope's tiny and tortured existence was now at hand. But ere it closed, it must close like Dryden's, characteristically, with an author's quarrel. Colley Cibber had long been a favourite of Pope's ire, and had as often retorted scorn, till at last, by laughing upon the stage at Pope's play (partly Gay's), entitled, "Three Hours After Marriage," he roused the bard almost to frenzy; and Pope set to work to remodel "The Dunciad;" and, dethroning Theobald, set up Cibber as the lawful King of the Dull, a most unfortunate substitution, since, while Theobald was the ideal of stolid, solemn stupidity, Cibber was gay, light, pert, and clever; full of pluck, too, and who overflowed in reply, with pamphlets which gave Pope both a headache and a heartache whenever he perused them.

Pope had never been strong, and for many years the variety and multitude of his frailties had been increasing. He had habitually all his life been tormented with headaches, for which he found the steam of strong coffee the chief remedy. He had hurt his stomach, too, by indulging in excess of stimulating viands, such as potted lampreys, and in copious and frequent drams. He was assailed at last by dropsy and asthma; and on the 30th of May 1744, he breathed his last, fifty-six years of age. He had long, he said, "been tired of the world," and died with philosophic composure and serenity. He took the sacrament according to the form of the Roman Catholic Church; but merely, he said, because it "looked right." A little before his death, he called for his desk, and began an essay on the immortality of the soul, and on those material things which tend to weaken or to strengthen it for immortality, enumerating generous wines as among the latter influences, and spirituous liquors among the former! His last words were, "There is nothing that is meritorious but virtue and friendship; and, indeed, friendship itself is only a part of virtue." Thus, "motionless and moanless," without a word about Christ—the slightest syllable of repentance—and with a scrap of heathen morality in his mouth, died the brilliant Alexander Pope. Who is ready to say, "May my last end be like his"? His favourite Martha Blount behaved, according to some accounts, with disgusting unconcern on the occasion. So true it is, "there is no friendship among the wicked," even although the heartless Bolingbroke, too, was by, and seems to have succeeded in squeezing out some crocodile tears, as he bent over the dying poet, and said, "O God! what is man?" His remains were, according to his wish, deposited in Twickenham church, near his parents, where the single letter P on the stone alone distinguishes the spot.

Pope's character, apart from his poetry, which we intend criticising in our next volume, was not specially interesting or elevated. He was a spoiled child, a small self-tormentor, full to bursting with petty spites, mean animosities, and unfounded jealousies. While he sought, with the fury of a pampered slave, to trample on those authors that were beneath him in rank or in popularity, he could on all occasions fawn with the sycophancy of a eunuch upon the noble, the rich, and the powerful. Hazlitt speaks of Moore as a "pug-dog barking from the lap of a lady of quality at inferior passengers." The description is far more applicable to Pope. We have much allowance to make for the influence exerted on his mind by his singularly crooked frame and sickly habit of body, by his position as belonging to a proscribed faith, and by his want of training in a public school; but after all these deductions, we cannot but deplore the spectacle of one of the finest, clearest, and sharpest minds that England ever produced, so frequently reminding you of a bright sting set in the body, and steeped in the venom, of a wasp. And yet, withal, he possessed many virtues, which endeared him to a multitude of friends. He was a kind son. He was a faithful and devoted friend. He loved, if not man, yet many men with deep tenderness. A keen politician he was not; but, so far as he went along with his party, he was true to the common cause. In morals, he was greatly superior, in point of external decorum, to most of the wits of the time; but in falsehood, finesse, treachery, and envy, he stood at the bottom of the list, without that plea of poverty, or wretchedness, or despair, which so many of them might have urged. Uneasy, indeed, he always, and unhappy he often, was; but very much of his uneasiness and unhappiness sprung from his own fault. He attacked others, and could not bear to be attacked in return. He was a bully and a coward. He threw himself into a thorn-hedge, and was amazed that he came out covered with scratches and blood. While he shone in satirising many kinds of vice, he laid himself open to retort by his own want of delicacy. He, as well as Swift, was fond of alluding in his verse to polluted and forbidden things. There, and there alone, his taste deserted him; and there is something disgusting and unnatural in the combination of the elegant and the obscene—the coarse in sentiment and the polished in style. And whatever may be said for many of the amiable traits of the Man, there is very little to be said for the general tendency—so far as healthy morality and Christian principle are concerned—of the writings of the Poet.

Alexander Pope – A Concise Bibliography

The Major works
Pastorals (1709)
An Essay on Criticism (1711)
Messiah (1712)
The Rape of the Lock (1712 and enlarged in 1714)
Windsor Forest (1713)
Translation of the Iliad (1715-1720)
Eloisa to Abelard (1717)
Three Hours After Marriage, with others (1717)
Elegy to the Memory of an Unfortunate Lady (1717)
The Works of Shakespear, in Six Volumes (1723-1725)

Translation of the Odyssey (1725-1726)
Peri Bathous, Or the Art of Sinking in Poetry (1727)
The Dunciad (1728)
Essay on Man (1733-1734)
The Prologue to the Satires (1735)

Printed in Great Britain
by Amazon